THESE TIMES, THIS PLACE
Muriel Gray

Edited by Moira Fors

We need good writers to tackle hard topics.
Maternity pay, public transport, gap year students,
poor housing – things that matter to us all. Muriel
Gray tells us why they do, and what needs to be
done. You might agree with her or you might
not – but you certainly won't be bored
when you read these articles from her regular
Sunday Herald column.

Muriel Gray began her media career in 1982
with Channel 4's music show *The Tube*. She went on
to present programmes such as *Frocks on the Box*, a
long running fashion series, and *Bliss*, a teenage
music and culture show. She has also presented
many Edinburgh Festival programmes, as well
as the *The Media Show* on Channel 4. She began
her own production company in 1987, now
part of IWC Media.

The first woman rector of Edinburgh University,
Muriel Gray is also a best selling author, with *The
First Fifty*, (a book about the Munro Mountains) and
three horror novels.

She lives in Glasgow with her husband and three
children. After her family, her other passions are
mountaineering, snowboarding and growing trees.

By the same author

Non Fiction
The First Fifty (Munro-bagging Without A Beard)

Fiction
The Trickster
Furnace
The Ancient

THESE TIMES, THIS PLACE
Muriel Gray

Edited by Moira Forsyth

SANDSTONE vista 6

The Sandstone Vista Series

These Times, This Place
First published 2005 in Great Britain by Sandstone Press Ltd
PO Box 5725, Dingwall, Ross-shire, IV15 9WJ, Scotland

The publisher acknowledges the financial support of both the
Highland Council, through the Education, Culture and Sport
Service, and the Literacies Initiative of the Highland
Community Learning and Development Strategy Partnership.

ISBN 0-9546333-7-7

The Sandstone Vista Series of books has
been written and skilfully edited
for the enjoyment of readers with differing levels
of reading skills, from the emergent to the accomplished.

Designed and typeset by Edward Garden Graphic Design,
Dingwall, Ross-shire, Scotland.

Printed and bound by Dingwall Printers Ltd,
Dingwall, Ross-shire, Scotland.

SANDSTONEPRESS
SCOTTISH LITERARY PUBLISHING HOUSE

www.sandstonepress.com

CONTENTS

INTRODUCTION

Muriel Gray is very much a woman of today. She has been in the public eye as a TV presenter since she first presented *The Tube* on Channel 4 in 1982. But she is now also well known as a talented writer of non-fiction as well as of horror novels. The articles in this collection show clearly her 'no-nonsense' thinking about matters that are important to us all.

The columns included in this book are taken from the *Sunday Herald* between November 2003 and August 2004. In them she takes a fresh look at maternity pay, public transport, gap-year students and social class. These are real issues for our time and place and Muriel brings clear thinking and sharp wit to all of them.

LEFT SPEECHLESS!

We're not really supposed to talk about class any more. You can tell that we're not because it's not aired in public, even when class is at the very centre of the debate.

Teenage pregnancies, for instance, are discussed in ways that would make you think a child having a baby at 15 is a problem that keeps all parents awake at night with worry, whether they are university-educated people living in wealthy suburbs or single parents on benefit in tower-blocks. It's not true. It's the same as with all social problems. Those most affected are those who are most disadvantaged. What we used to call the working class.

The way people are divided up is so much more complex than it used to be in the first half of the 20th century. Perhaps that's what makes talking about class seem old fashioned. For instance, 'working class' used to refer to the exploited workers who laboured without profiting from their hard graft. But that doesn't apply to people who've never worked and are the second or even third generation of their family living on benefit. To label such people an 'underclass' is ugly and insulting. It's almost inhumane.

The term 'working class' seems old fashioned and wrong. But whatever the politically correct words we use to define the people who have the least, the class system is still very much with us. It might be a bit more fluid around the edges but pretending it doesn't exist is pointless.

Take for instance the recent report which was concerned that 'young people' can no longer communicate. It says that because they can't talk clearly in good English, they are failing dismally in almost every aspect of life. This is not true. What the report means, but doesn't say, is that it's working-class youths who are communicating more poorly than before.

Middle-class youngsters are doing what they always did. They're busy using the English language to their own benefit. They're debating in their comfortable schools, colleges and universities. Then they're going on to pick and choose their career paths as a result. It was ever thus. How well they communicate is of little interest to anyone, particularly me.

What has changed is that the working class used to be able to communicate perfectly well, and now they can't. This bothers me enormously, as does the worrying fact that such reports are too politically correct to deal with it head on. Some of our greatest thinkers, speakers and far-seeing politicians have been solidly working class. Sometimes the local accents, the way they spoke, may not have pleased some of their class-ridden enemies. But they way they spoke didn't stand in the way of the message they had to convey. In fact, the very richness of their speech was part of their power.

A recent television re-run showed Jimmy Reid inflaming his fellow workers with political passion. They heard his outstanding speeches, then vox pops of young workers as they left the meeting. They were in their late teens and early 20s. They had the same accent as Reid, the same glottal stops and flattened vowels, and used the same imperfect grammar. Yet they were united in the fact that they were all very articulate. They were well able to speak for themselves and had wide vocabularies. Compare this with the average modern working-class youth. Their new speak is admittedly interesting, not least because there is now a clear male/female divide. For the males the words are spoken largely on an out-breath, with the word 'man' peppered everywhere. They usually speak nasally, their voices rising and falling like a Californian dialect. Females, who rarely or never use the word 'man', speak mostly in a monotone, their voices rising at the end of each sentence.

There's nothing wrong with these contemporary accents, since the way language develops is always exciting. But there is something that marks them out as different from everything that's gone before. Both male and female ways of speaking are very inarticulate and short on vocabulary. It's not snobbery to point out that it's these youths the report is referring to, and not the Alasdairs and Fionas making points of order at their schools' debating contests. It's simply fact. Stanley Baxter and Billy Connolly may have mocked the speech of their grandparents, but those grandparents could still express anger and passion - enough to bring down governments and shape society. It's also fact that this new dialect is a terrible handicap to those who have no other way of communicating. It means they remain silent, invisible, without the power to change their lives.

The men and women in the Scottish Socialist Party are proud to be called working class. But you notice that none of them talk in this fashion. They have normal, attractive working-class accents. They are articulate and expressive. Thankfully, they can dive into the fray and be heard.

They should be as anxious as anyone that this huge section of Scotland's youth is being tied down by not being able to communicate. Without an improvement in this basic skill, these youngsters will end up with 'careers' grunting behind the counters of fast-food restaurants. What's more, they are the next generation of adults, who will have limited choices and uncertain futures. We desperately need to hear them, and to do that we have to give them a way of expressing themselves. A way that means everyone can understand what the hell it is they're saying. Man.

16th November, 2003

OUR REAL SHAME – OUR HOUSES

My Dad's parents used to live in a slum in Glasgow's Maryhill. It didn't seem unusual at the time. Lots of people did. I used to visit them when I was a child. They had a two-room tenement flat with no inside toilet. The main entertainment was standing on a box at the kitchen sink to watch the rats scurry about in the back-court midden outside the window. The toilet next to the midden was used by six families, and you took your own toilet roll in with you. The smell was awful. We always had to clap our hands loudly before opening the door. This was to scare away the rats that might be hiding behind the cracked toilet bowl.

My grandmother was finally moved out of this stupid place in 1978. She got a flat in a new skyscraper. It did have some social problems, but it was clean and dry. No rats. And a lovely bathroom, of course.

So there we are. The bad old days were swept away. We used to put up with people living in terrible houses and then Scotland finally got civilised and did something about it. Well done us. At least that's what I thought. Two weeks ago I sat in a conference hall in Edinburgh. I slid down in my seat, feeling horror and shame at my country. The Scottish Federation of Housing Associations (SFHA) showed a video to launch a campaign for new homes we desperately need.

We saw a man with motor neurone disease. He can hardly walk but he can't get re-housed. And yet he lives in a narrow house on many floors. The stairs made a visit to the toilet a major event. He's a prisoner in his own home.

We also heard about a family with a daughter in a wheelchair. She's severely disabled, but they live in a flat at the top of a long flight of concrete steps. They'd be hard for Chris Bonington to climb. They carry the little girl up in their arms while she's still small enough to make this possible. Then they bump the heavy wheelchair up behind them.

Anything on the council house list for them? No. Hundreds ahead of them. Housing association? No properties available.

Then there was the extended family of 10 newly settled immigrants. They are working hard to make their tiny high-rise flat cope with so many bodies. They are struggling to try and find a spare corner for the children to do homework. It's hard to find somewhere for those who have jobs to get a little sleep, when others in the family are still awake. It's like some grim modern-day version of the Broons. But they're living in a space much smaller than Glebe Street and without the gags. It went on and on. We saw photographs of evil slums with holes in the floor for toilets, which are still housing families with small children.

We saw young people in rural areas living in freezing caravans. The houses in their area have been sold to second-home owners. No new council houses are being built to replace the ones sold off privately. And of course we saw what little relief there is for the long-term homeless. The point of telling us about this misery was that the government has currently agreed to build just

4500 new homes for rent each year. The SFHA insists this is miles short of the figure needed just to do something about the present crisis. It will go nowhere to stop the problem growing, as clearly it will. They insist that a minimum of 10,000 new homes are needed every year, or people will continue to suffer the misery I have described.

What the hell has gone wrong here? The Fraser Inquiry has been looking at whether we should have a grand vision for a public building in a small country, our new Parliament. At the same time, we seem to be sitting on our backsides and denying modern Scots a basic human right. The right to live in houses that suit their needs and allow them a little dignity. The huge sell-off of council houses which started in the 1980s happened with no new buildings to replace them. It doesn't take much of a brain to see this was always going to cause major social problems.

Of course our housing associations are great. The fact they had to be created at all is not something we should be proud of. But we need them to make up for the government doing nothing to provide cheap, well built and well planned housing. Now that they've become a vital part of Scotland's housing programme, the least the government can do is bloody well listen to them when they have something important to say.

Decent homes are the starting point for civilised society. Crime, health, poor education, unemployment and plain ordinary despair all lead back to bad housing. The government baulks at the cost of creating these desperately needed new homes. But they should look at the huge cost of the problems caused by poor housing. As usual, other European countries put us to shame on this front. Why, with our recent history of slum clearances, do we appear to have learned nothing? No wonder we're uncomfortable with the Fraser Inquiry going on about a global vision for the Parliament.

Why should people in modern Scotland, such as the ones in the SFHA's video, struggle to get by in appalling conditions? Why should they be prisoners in their own homes? In conditions like these, they will never live fulfilling lives. It's not much of a vision for a new Parliament. Not much of a beacon for Scotland's future.

7th December 2003

WHOSE FAULT IS IT IF THE KIDS ARE FAT?

What would the press do without the regular supply of health scares to report? You know the kind of thing: 'Low birth-weight babies less likely to buy caravans' or, 'New report shows women over 40 who put sweeteners in their tea are the main cause of religious intolerance.' This nonsense is very annoying to people of my generation. After all, we were raised on Angel Delight, Smash powdered potato and Vesta curry washed down with Vimto. We had tobacco smoke constantly blown into our little lungs by every adult in every walk of life. Our health was not the main concern in the 1950s and 1960s. Yet somehow we survived despite all of this. We also walked to school by ourselves from the age of five, and we were tipped out of the house at weekends to roam about. Then we came home to watch as much television (even if it was black and white) as we wished.

So how did it happen that this same generation can buy organic popcorn in public without blushing? How come they think children will be attacked by paedophiles the minute they're out of their NASA-tested car seats? When did we get this fearful? Of course we're talking mainly here about the middle class. The working class and upper class have a more basic approach to raising their kids. The parents may be from opposite ends of the social scale, but both wee Kylie and little Torquil will have to fend for themselves as soon as they're out of nappies. Then their parents can get on with struggling on benefits or shooting pheasants in Yorkshire.

It's only the soppy middle classes who think chocolate is dangerous. Or that children's birthdays have to end with five quid party bags or it's practically child abuse. These 'health' reports are aimed at them, tickling their fears and making them feel guilty.

Take, for instance, the latest scare story. Glasgow University carried out a study of 78 three-year-olds. Apparently, they found that, on average, the children spent only 20 to 25 minutes per day being active. The fault was that children now spend more time than ever watching television. This is, it should be said, a worthwhile study. In the battle against child obesity it's no doubt useful. But of course it's not the study but the reporting of it that's as silly as ever.

This data could be used to find out why many parents - particularly low-income parents in poor housing - can't make sure their children are active. But no, parents are blamed yet again. Parents must be educated!

Hoi, you! Yes, Fatty, you! Don't you know that plonking your kids in front of the telly is really bad for them?

My wild guess is that, yes, most parents of toddlers do know it, but there's not much they can do. Let's say you live in a high-rise flat with a dodgy lift and drug dealers around the stairwell. Let's suppose there's not a square foot of green space within walking distance of that flat. Well, not one that's free of yobs or not littered with dog-poo and needles.

Just what would you do? Take them swimming? Er, where? What if you've got another pre-school child and a baby? Local toddler gym club? How many of those are there in deprived areas?

I don't know what sort of families the report studied. But toddlers who go to state nurseries are leaping and bounding around most of the day. So, not them. If you show a toddler a lawn and a ball it will run and tumble until it drops. So not people with decent back gardens or people near lovely parks. So we must be talking about people who are trapped by where they live. Not people who refuse to be 'educated'.

This misleading reporting of health research is a way of covering up real problems. Problems which could be fixed. Give families decent houses with gardens and their children will be healthier. Give people opportunities and choices and they will be healthier. Don't let developers build over every square inch of urban space. Start building parks and playing fields. Then people will be healthier. When did you last hear of a new park being made? Stop letting the wicked food industry tell us what to eat. Then, yes, people will be healthier.

We don't need bloody educating, thanks very

much. Everyone knows that smoking, drinking and eating fatty foods are bad for you. Maybe they're not having steamed vegetables for dinner and doing advanced yoga. But it could be because of where they live. And the way they have to live. Not because they need 'educating'.

We need the big problems solved if we want a happier and healthier Britain. We're ignoring the real victims, who are unhealthy because they're poor. Instead we're just putting out scare stories to smug middle-class parents. And that will get us nowhere. The small consolation is that such parents' heads are so far up their own backsides no one can hear them scream.

18th January, 2004

WHY OPERA DOESN'T HAVE TO
MAKE YOU CRY

I have always loved one very silly scene, one of many, in the film *Pretty Woman*. Richard Gere plays a lonely millionaire who has hired a prostitute for the week. He starts to fall for her and keeps testing her out to see what kind of person she is. The big challenge is when he takes her to see an opera. He tells her that if opera enters your soul the first time you see it, it will be there forever. If not, you will learn to appreciate it, but you will never love it. Or something like that anyway.

Of course we all know that the pretty prostitute will 'get it' as soon as the curtain goes up. (Understanding opera I mean, of course, and not just another rogering from her handsome client.) And so she does. Tears well in her eyes at the closing aria, and she has passed the test. It has entered her soul. Of course the millionaire's theory about opera is utter bollocks, and so indeed is the entire film. However, it is another example of the popular idea that high art is very difficult. Shallow idiots will never be able to appreciate it no matter how hard they try.

That's Hollywood of course, and we shouldn't take it terribly seriously. But a real encounter I had a couple of years ago was more chilling. I was about to appear on some programme or other with Anne Taylor, at that time a government minister. We started talking about education and she railed against the idea that children were still being forced to read Shakespeare. 'What the hell does Shakespeare mean to a bunch of kids in Middlesborough?' she demanded, clearly expecting agreement.

I asked her if she had been taught Shakespeare. Er, yes. And then gone to university? Er, yes again. Ah, well then Anne. You've had the benefit of the Bard, but by all means keep the Middlesborough kids nice and dumb why don't you? After all you're going to need someone to pack your groceries at the checkout before you give a dinner party. It's best not to muddle them up with what Shakespeare is about, while they struggle to unfold a cardboard wine-bottle carrier.

Unfortunately she's not the only one to speak such rubbish in politics, Hollywood, or indeed society at large. The idea that what is popular is better than 'high art' is an idea that is called 'realism'. It is also an idea that sucks. A survey conducted by *The Herald* last week suggested that most Scots believe the funding of art for art's sake is a waste of money. They think every grant for the arts should be valued only if it can be measured. In other words, if it creates more jobs, it's educational, or it brings in more money from tourists.

Poor old Scottish Opera, with all its money woes, came in for a particular hammering. The public, it seems, prefers traditional music instead of music written by long dead Italians. We know this already. If not, then Scottish Opera would have to play every night, plus matinees, for the thousands who wanted tickets. Meanwhile Celtic Connections and the World Pipe Band Championships would play to tumbleweed blowing across an empty Glasgow Green.

Surely successful cultures are diverse cultures. Scottish Opera and Scottish Ballet have little trouble filling their performances. There are plenty of people aching to see what they have to offer. The trouble is the huge difference in cost. Maintaining a company, putting on the production with its sets, costumes, musicians and rehearsals is a huge cost. There's a large gulf between that and buying some real ale and paying for the van rental for five bearded men with fiddles.

I have much sympathy with the public view on Scotland's native music. I was lucky enough to have been at the first (and so far only) performance by the newly formed Scottish National Youth Pipe Band. Words can't describe the sheer pleasure of that wonderful show. There's no question that if public funding is needed to keep those young people together then sackfuls of money should be thrown at them. But do we really have to choose? Surely the question is not between high art and popular or traditional art. Surely the question is this. Should we be finding and committing more money and support for the whole damned thing, right across the board?

Of course there has to be quality control. Nobody wants to see money chucked away on half-baked, piss poor theatre. Plays about the miners' strike being trawled round community centres, or Norwegian artists making videos of themselves. But can we really not afford to fund both? That is, the popular entertainment which the public wants, as well as opera, ballet and theatre. Opera, ballet and theatre have a much smaller fan base. But they enrich us in different ways, which are just as valid. If that's the case, then let's hear the government say it out loud. Tell us. Have the courage to say: 'Look, we're not prepared to pay for a rich, diverse culture, and so you'll have to choose. High or low? Traditional or classical?'

What's clear is that the Scottish Executive can't, despite all it says, make the arts part of education, social inclusion and 'access' if we only have one kind of art.

Who knows what the government really has in mind? Maybe before they decide, the Culture Minister should round up some prostitutes, take them to Scottish Opera and see if they cry. If they do it might be because, despite his many charms, they'll have noticed he's not Richard Gere.

25th January, 2004

THE READING HABIT

Childhood memories are strange things. Children's brains are strange. Parents pay thousands of pounds to take their children to Disneyland. Then they find out later that their children remember almost nothing about it but can still recall every second of a rainy visit to Fort William. My own example is just as odd. Some of my most precious childhood moments are of visiting libraries, both in Dumfries and then in Glasgow where I spent the most of my youth.

You might think this daft. A public library is hardly on a par with a trip to the magic plastic kingdom of Disney. The library had no hair-raising rides and you couldn't shake hands with poorly paid workers dressed as cartoon characters. Instead, there was simply the heady delight of pushing through creaking doors out of the biting cold and going into overheated, brightly lit rooms packed with colourful books. The old radiators hissed and the smell of floor wax filled the nostrils. I went into the children's section to choose whatever I wanted, while my parents browsed the adult shelves.

These were contented times. Part of the joy was that none of the beautiful books I chose to take home would cost my parents a thing. They were absolutely free. Unfortunately, I didn't become all that well read since, in Dumfries, I borrowed the same book - *Toffle and The Moomins* - for over a year. Every fortnight I went back to renew its stamp. Then in Glasgow's Partick Library I usually borrowed poorly written ghost stories. But browsing, being alone in the peaceful atmosphere, was so wonderful it stayed with me. Regardless of my poor choices of books, it introduced me to the idea that reading was a lifelong pleasure.

So when a brand new library opened near us recently, our family were enrolled in it before the paint dried. To my enormous satisfaction, the children seem to love being in a library as much as I did.

It's therefore gloomy to read that Audit Scotland says that libraries are in decline across the country. Apparently the proportion of the population that borrows books from libraries fell, for the fifth year running, to just over 24%. There are success stories. Glasgow is the most notable with an increase of borrowing up 7%. But the general pattern in the country as a whole shows that libraries are simply not pulling in the punters the way they used to.

Of course, with any failure, the finger of blame waves madly around in an attempt to find out whose fault it is. There are obvious targets. The internet is taking over from the written word as the way to access knowledge. Bookshops now provide comfy seats where you can browse the stock in peace, unless your trousers are tied up with string and you smell of pee. One true and sad reason is that people are becoming less literate. But it strikes me that this last reason hasn't much to do with borrowing habits at libraries.

This week we've learned that children's writer Jacqueline Wilson has toppled Catherine

Cookson from her position as the author people borrow most. The rest of the list includes writers like Danielle Steel. It's safe to say then, that it's children who borrow most books. And they're followed by adults less hungry for literature than for piles of bodice-ripping crap.

But if libraries are not full of people who want serious books, they are still visited by a huge variety of the public. They all enjoy reading, and they all have the opportunity to put down the Catherine Cookson and pick up more demanding or difficult literature, even if they never do it. This seems to be something Glasgow has understood. They have acted on it brilliantly. Get us into the library by any means. Then we will not only enjoy the experience, but it's pretty certain that a great many more of us will read.

Our new library is a perfect example. It's bright, modern, cheerful and has banks of computers. Some of them are connected to the internet and some are simply for children to play games on. It lends DVDs, videos and CDs as well as books. It has a cheery children's area often with storytellers or puppets. There are events to keep toddlers amused while parents use computers or sit down to read. In short, it's just a lovely place to be. What's more it has had an effect on the surrounding area. This corner of the city used to be shabby. Now it has a sense of revival and community purpose.

In a similar way, the downstairs library at Glasgow's Gallery of Modern Art provides a completely free haven in the city centre. Computers are available and books and newspapers can be read while you're drinking a coffee. Glasgow has proved that if you provide decent facilities people will use them and we, and the community in general, will benefit greatly.

So why aren't other councils following suit, if the numbers of people using their libraries has fallen?

Updating and refurbishing libraries ticks a hell of a lot more boxes than simply providing free romantic novels to those who enjoy bodice-rippers. Libraries introduce pre-school children into the world of reading. They provide thinking space for those who have nowhere else. At the same time they can be stimulating and exciting. They're even social meeting places, where local events can be advertised and a broad range of people can be reached.

The book-borrowing bit is a red herring. Although reading is at the heart of it all, a modern library is much more than the sum of its parts. To let them go because not so many people are borrowing books would be a disaster for Scotland. Let Glasgow's example be a blueprint for the future, not just a one-off success.

15th February, 2004

PUSHING GRANNY OFF THE BUS

What fun watching Michael Howard trying to reinvent his Party. The Party that used to be famous for being full of villains is now full of caring and liberal people. It's not so long since the Conservatives' views on immigration and race meant anyone with a face darker than Coco the Clown was seen as a threat. So it was hilarious to watch Howard lecturing the people of Burnley recently. He was there to warn them of the wicked ways of the nasty BNP, that ugly right-wing party. Mind you, the voters of Burnley have elected a few of the BNP as councillors.

Even more surprising, Howard has now decided to put behind him that old Conservative idea that single mothers are dangerous. He was making a big effort to win the nursing mothers' vote. A Conservative government would pay mothers to stay at home for three years and look after their children instead of returning to work. This is what happens in Finland, where mothers are paid £150 per month to stay at home with the first child, and another £50 for every other child. Parents on the poverty line get an extra £100, but the basic rate is paid to all, however well off they are.

Let's forget for a moment that the Tories are desperate. They would clearly say or do anything to get a sniff of power again. Let's look at this new attempt to win public support. They're not alone in thinking that taking care of working mothers is a vote winner. The Government is also thinking about childcare. No doubt it hopes to save some votes from those who are still disgusted with Labour after the disaster of Blair's war on Iraq.

Clearly both parties think it essential that the taxpayer is responsible for bringing up children in families where parents need or wish to work. What has not been examined in any great detail is *why*. A decent society, when it works, can certainly do good for its people even when the motives are selfish. For instance, a very rich but bitter person might still see the sense in subsidising the poor, even though he despises them. If he does, the community he lives in may have less crime and his quality of life will be improved. The tax he pays to fund education and support the poor are just as effective, even if he's willing to give it for the wrong reasons.

So when it comes to the taxpayer subsidising parenting, there must be benefits for all, or else it's hard to justify. So what are the benefits? Let's take Fiona and Simon. Fiona is a nurse and her partner Simon sells electrical goods in a superstore. When they choose to have a child, why would it benefit us for Fiona to take three state-paid years off to look after it? We paid for her training and we need her skills more than we need Simon selling us dodgy insurance on washing machines. And why should we subsidise them at all? It might be hard to juggle two jobs. And if they choose childcare over living on a single income they'll still be broke, like most new parents. But they will have the joy of a baby, and like everyone else they'll work something out. Why should the taxpayer make their life easier? If their child is healthy then there's not a great deal wrong with their lives. But there are thousands of other people screaming for financial help who need it far more.

Now take Anne. She's a single mother with two children by different fathers. Neither of the fathers is around. She's poor, uneducated, the child of a family that has been on benefit for three generations. It's not her fault she's rubbish at parenting. She's young, immature and has never had a good role model. Is it better for society, and Anne, to pay for her to stay at home on her own, depressed, and smoking in front of the telly all day for three years? Her kids screaming the place down, probably. Or would it be better to try and get her out to work, give her training and self-esteem, and her own money? And her kids would be well cared for by professionals.

Then there's Emma. She's a lawyer and her husband is an accountant. What possible benefit does the taxpayer get if Emma decides to take three years off? If she's paid by the state to fanny about having morning coffee with her pals and reading books on a park bench beside the swings? This notion of blanket, across-the-board childcare help doesn't make sense. What's more, why is being a parent seen as being more important than being a single, childless person looking after a sick or elderly relative? After all, that's not a choice but a duty.

Howard changes colour like a chameleon. He might think just now that this bandwagon will win votes, but he should be careful. Having a child is a lifestyle choice, not a right. Not everyone believes that the parents of healthy bouncing babies are the most down-trodden victims in society. Women certainly need more help and positive action to become more equal in the workplace, but that includes childless women and not just mothers.

The issues that are keeping women back are a lot more complex than just the question of who looks after the kids. Why should Emma sip her Starbucks coffee on our tax while someone's 75-year-old disabled mum still hasn't got a home help?

22nd February, 2004

THE HOME GROWN POOR ARE MUCH LESS EXOTIC

Gap-year students abroad. Don't we love 'em? I met a memorable one years ago in Nigeria. As we ended our work in Lagos, colleagues and I were propping up the bar of the Hilton hotel. This is a building ringed by armed guards to keep out the riff-raff. We were quickly joined by two middle-aged Yorkshire men and by one lanky Home Counties youth. The boy was ending his gap year in Africa, treating himself to a final drink before heading to the airport for his flight home.

Thinking he was broke, we bought the youth his drinks. But we regretted this later when my colleague spotted him checking his flight on his club class air ticket. After a few beers, he began bragging about his uncovering of the real Africa. Middle-class fools, like the ones paying for his drinks, knew nothing of the real Africa.

We quizzed him politely. It turned out he had done no more than backpack around the continent taking photographs of cattle and ragged children. His biggest thrill was attending a tribal wedding in Chad and getting smashed on a local brew made from bean husks. Puffed up with importance, he demanded to know whether the two Yorkshiremen had ever been to Chad. They said they had not. He snorted with contempt. He could see we were just ignorant, Hilton people. He was a traveller. He'd been to an African wedding, for pity's sake! What would we ever learn by hiding in five-star hotels?

We were all relieved when he left for his plane. Then we found out the two men were engineers who had been working all over Africa, if not Chad, for the best part of 15 years. They worked for a company helping to bring clean water to small townships and villages. They had been living with the locals for months on end in the same mud huts and compounds.

Both men could speak Ibo and Yoruba fluently. They had had amazing adventures, and were passionate about Africa and its people. Sadly our gap-year student missed all of this information. We pictured him already at 35,000 feet, laying off to someone in the next seat about the real Africa, failing to notice his fellow passenger was Nelson Mandela.

This may seem a bit cruel. After all, who hasn't been an utter dick at the tender age of 18? But I was reminded of this when I read about Prince Harry's gap-year trip to Africa, echoing his big brother's trip to Chile. The result has been a mad rush among the middle class to follow the royal example. Now they're sending their pre-university teenagers to help needy foreigners and provide years of dinner-party chat on their return.

It would be unkind and untrue to imagine that Prince Harry is getting nothing at all out of being with the orphans of Aids victims. And I'm sure he's not there just for royal PR purposes. But there is something disturbing about this new Grand Tour. The well-heeled now think their young people must have it to develop their minds and characters.

In the 19th century the rich sent their kids around Europe to look at art whether they liked it or not. But what I find hard to take is the way parents these days are just following another fashion: they're packing off their teenagers to look at the poor.

The theory is that the youths, by 'helping' in poor communities, will come back with compassion and wisdom which will stand them in good stead for that future career as lawyer, banker or businessperson. So many people want to do this now that there are at least 50 organisations offering 'package' gap years, which appeal to parents and future employers. But Kate Simpson, from the School of Geography, Politics and Sociology at the University of Newcastle, points out that they're not much use to the communities the students travel to.

Ms Simpson did some research into gap-year students abroad. She says communities have been bombarded with 18-year-olds who are worse than useless. They paint houses without consulting the owners; they teach, they build, and they even deliver babies, without the experience or skills they need to do so safely and well. She says: 'You need a gap year to become successful. It is now part of becoming employable, as necessary as A-levels and a degree.'

So it would seem that what was just a fad has changed into a sort of education which helps you help others. It's now a status symbol, and a way of padding out your CV. And it doesn't even help the poor. Thankfully the government's plan to fund gap years for poorer UK students means they'll do voluntary work here in unglamorous Britain. Tasks like working with the disabled or restoring facilities in their own areas.

That's a bit more like it. That shows you don't have to travel to exotic places to understand people who are less fortunate, or indeed do something to help them. But helping at home will just be for poorer students and piddling about abroad in fancy hats will be the lot of the rich. So there will be even more CV status for students who have gone overseas.

Teaching compassion to young people by example, and making sure they can do some good, will always be worthwhile. But when charity is self-serving, and when it exploits other people, the words of Jean-Paul Sartre come to mind: 'The poor don't know that they're there to show how generous we are.'

7th March, 2004

THE REAL TERROR ON PUBLIC TRANSPORT

I can't stomach it any more. Anyone commenting on the news, in anything from *Ringtones Monthly* to *The Guardian,* should be writing only about the war between militant, fundamentalist Islam and the rest of the world. But it's getting very hard to find sane answers in the face of the last few weeks' nauseating events.

The madmen who bombed Madrid got the changes they wanted. On the back of that success, the barking mad fundamentalists are now attacking France. They threaten that the country will see 'blood running to its borders' - and why? As a punishment for making little girls in France feel equal at school by keeping headscarves for outside and not inside the classroom. This is in spite of the fact that France shouted loudest in opposition to the Iraq war. Ah, yes, the logic of the religious nutter.

Here's another worrying thing - though it was meant to reassure us. The leader of a Spanish Muslim community expressed worries about anti-Muslim feeling. He meant to put our minds at rest by saying that Islam never, ever, sanctions 'unjust killings'. Do you notice a rogue word in that statement? Unjust? Not just simply 'killings'? Ok, those who don't believe in God do, sometimes, cherry-pick morsels of morality from all those religions out there. So I suppose you can hardly blame some of them for thinking 'thou shalt not kill' means not ever, ever, ever. In other words, it doesn't mean that sometimes Allah thinks it's ok for his followers to snuff out the odd person who was frankly begging for it.

But like I said, I don't want to think about this any more. I don't want to think about how the West has actually prevented the reform of Islam. I don't want to think about how it has helped push Muslim countries into extremes by threatening them with alien beliefs as much as with arms. I don't want to think about how that leads to the mad spread of hate and fear and grief in the name of a God, not even a cause. I don't want to think about the terrorist attack that is going to happen soon in a British city.

Nor do I want to think about the millions of honest, decent Muslim people of Europe. The ones who hate all killing, just or unjust. They just want to get on with their lives like everyone else, raising their children in peace and building their futures. But now they have to suffer the active dislike of non-Muslims who don't understand what's going on and fear them.

No. Instead I want to talk about rude Glasgow bus drivers.

Not relevant enough for you right now? Well you're very wrong. In fact our own dear sister paper *The Herald* has been going on about it for most of last week. This is since a Dr Masaru Araki met a downright rude bus driver on a trip in Glasgow and wrote to the paper to say how disgusted he was. Since then the *Herald* postbag has bulged with this weighty topic. Other people have written in with their own bad experiences. Even a fed-up bus driver has given his well-argued point of view. He points out we can't expect anything else from private bus companies that treat their employees with as much contempt as their customers.

The most depressing thing the driver said, however, was how revolting we are as passengers. This is hard to argue with. I like the bus. I use it often. The last trip was no different from usual. I was scowled at by the driver for fumbling with my change and daring to ask a question about where exactly the bus might take me. And of course he ignored the question. But just as the bus driver who wrote to the *Herald* said, this short journey, like so many others, was not without incident.

In the space of 20 minutes a young mother with a buggy called the driver a 'fat tosser'. Two youths, as they got off the bus, threw their soft drink cans at him, laughing as they fizzed and bounced off the thin Perspex shield that protects the driver from people like us. We passengers, like the driver, ignored these incidents, because they're the norm and not the exception.

Maybe bad-tempered bus drivers are letting us down and ruining our tourist industry. But the bigger truth is that it's the public who moulds the driver. Us. We horrify and repulse the tourist on a far greater scale than one surly man behind the wheel. Probably he can't wait for his shift to end when he can escape the contempt of the public and his employers. He wants to go home to put his feet up and watch innocent people being blown apart on 24-hour news.

Damn. Sorry. Slipped up there. Was hoping the bus driver thing would turn out to be funny. I suppose it comes back to that cherry-picking from religion. I like the one that insists we're personally responsible for all our actions, that we must forgive, and that everyone deserves our love. It means loving innocent people on commuter trains as well as surly bus drivers. If we take it to the extreme, it means bombers as well. Tricky.

21st March, 2004

DOES MUM REALLY KNOW BEST?

The professional classes grumble that they have lost their status in society. Lawyers, judges, teachers, generals and majors, doctors and nurses, are no longer respected the way they were in the past. Some argue that this is a bad thing for society.

The truth, however, is that there is still plenty of public respect for professionals. But now it's not granted just because they have qualifications. The professionals now have to work hard to prove they deserve respect. This is surely better than the days when the masses had to doff their caps to people with letters after their name.

After all the court cases we've heard about which prove the medical profession to be at fault, no one thinks Doctor Knows Best any more. We know too that judges can let their personal feelings get in the way. And as for the military? Er, best left at the moment, don't you think?

We know of bad teachers, cruel nurses, useless this and hopeless that. So we're not so ready to believe in our professional classes. But we are now able to recognise first rate work, dedication and skill when we see it. This is particularly true when we see it in sharp contrast to work that's badly done. It means that those who deserve our praise and admiration get it. Those who don't, feel the cold wind of our disdain.

But there is still an area where ability doesn't matter. These people are given respect anyway. It's when the media use the term 'parent'. In the world of the tabloids, 'parent' or the terms 'mum' and 'dad' are words that imply much more than simply being part of a family. When an ordinary woman has her photo in a red-top in a story of good luck or bad, if she has children she is always 'mum'. For example: 'Mum-of-three was thrown from bus by thugs.' If her children were not there at the time, then the fact that she is a mother has nothing to do with the story. It doesn't mean any more than if she were also a member of a fishing club. 'Keen angler thrown from bus by thugs' does not have quite the same impact.

The title 'mum' is there to grant the woman increased social status. It's supposed to make us feel more for her. If it turns out one of the thugs is also a parent, we're not likely to hear this. 'Mum', in this common example, means she should get respect, and the tabloids are very fussy when deciding who should get this gift.

Given this rule, we have no excuse for not noticing it in the papers this week. We've been reading acres of print about a woman complaining that her 14-year-old daughter's abortion was carried out without her knowing about it or agreeing. This mum has been making a great deal of noise about how badly she's been affected by finding this out. She's calling for the law to be changed so that minors won't be able to keep this sort of health issue confidential.

There's no need to keep reminding us she is a 'mum'. After all, the story's about her daughter and their relationship, so it hardly takes a genius to work out that she is a mother. Once again the word is there to remind us of her status. It reminds us she is morally superior.

The tabloids getting mad at the professionals

and the school who helped to refer the pregnant girl ignore the fact that this woman has behaved appallingly. She has such a poor relationship with her unfortunate daughter that the child has had unprotected sex. She's then looked for advice and help from strangers rather than her own mother. But the mother has also chosen to reveal her daughter's name and parade her ordeal in the national and international press.

Many people see this mother as irresponsible and self-centred. But that takes a very poor second place in the tabloid world to the fact that she is an 'angry mum'. Angry mums, as we know, are always right.

The tabloids assume the professionals - the teachers and health workers - are wicked people, working away with their own agenda to corrupt and ruin young lives. The 'mum', for whom of course we have respect, is a brave crusader.

It's very strange to assume that the way someone's body works, to create a child, means that they should in some way have higher social standing. Some may consider this woman a very poor parent. Yet her flawed judgment is being held up as better than that of the school counsellor who assisted the daughter in her decision. The counsellor, who is apparently hounding this young woman, is only 21, but most significantly, she is not a mum. How can a non-mum possibly know better than an angry mum?

The whole affair is that the mother has been seeking publicity, using the tragedy of her daughter's predicament. And of course the pro-lifers, like flies to a dung-heap, are now howling in protest. They're even picketing the school where it all began. Happily, the law will not change, as it exists for very sound reasons. It has survived a challenge already from the smug Victoria Gillick, another 'angry mum' seeking publicity.

Perhaps what should be put in place is a law that could prevent parents from using their children in this manner, and stop tabloid newspapers profiting from such stupidity.

16th May, 2004

THE END OF THE WORLD, STUPID?

There are many ways in which our doomed species will meet its inevitable end. Some of them, like ice ages and meteorites, are entertaining. The end of the world because of population explosion or nuclear war is less appealing. After all, that would be our own fault.

Hollywood shows how the world might end in films like the new and very silly global warming epic, *The Day After Tomorrow*. But the end will doubtless come through something less glamorous than giant tidal waves or crumbling ice caps. We are most likely to die of stupidity. No - one cannot really die of stupidity, in the same way that signs on the motorway telling us that 'tiredness can kill' are misleading. It is not tiredness that kills, but the fact that tiredness can cause the sort of crashes that kill - our internal organs pierced by high-speed metal.

It's the results of stupidity that will do for us, rather than the stupidity itself. Otherwise, the streets would be littered with the bodies of those who had simply keeled over and died of being too stupid. The casualties after an Orange Walk or a BNP rally, for example, would be huge. But the results of our own stupidity came to mind while walking around the battlefield of Hastings earlier last week. I was with a defence correspondent and a keen historian.

These clever people mused on many things, including the changing face of warfare. Whereas Harold and William slogged it out in a battle that started at 9a.m. sharp and stuck to agreed rules, modern warfare is clearly more complex. What has not changed is the fact that then, just as now, people behaved like morons. Kings and conquerors slogged it out, all believing that some god or other wanted them to win.

The men with the swords died horribly, doing what they were told, for the same reasons. Torture and brutality were standard. Decency was a luxury that did not apply when people were doing their god's will. The peasants who waited in their villages, fearing the news, only wanted a peaceful life. They wanted to get back to working, eating, sleeping, breeding and thinking about very little.

Does any of this sound familiar? It would be comforting to say that the violence of the past was because people didn't have a grasp of basic science. They didn't understand the universe, or even the facts of biology. But if that's the case, how do we forgive modern man for being bone-headed? The average citizen in 1066 had a number of beliefs. He believed that foreigners were inferior and to be treated with suspicion. He believed that menopausal women were witches who should be burnt. And he thought there was a god who was always on his side. Readers of our tabloid press can read just the same views written down right now. So why are we still idiots?

A senior geneticist suggested last year that there has always been the same ratio of pea-brained people to smart ones. This caused some controversy.

He said the ratio of pea-brained to smart people could never change, however well educated and civilised we became. All that changes through history is the way in which a tiny number of wise people sway the huge number of daft ones. In a dark age the clever people have been silenced. In a golden age their ideas and advances are given power. His examples in history showed this happening over and over.

It's not hard to see why such a theory was controversial. Such a gloomy view hardly sits well with our own ideas of civilisation and progress. Some might even claim it borders on fascism. But his point was that breeding people for intelligence is fruitless. The clever pop up at random, if much more rarely than the stupid. However, historians don't agree on the core reasons for many of the world's good and bad times. So how can we be sure it was always the brainboxes doing the right thing and the dim doing the wrong?

After all, cleverness and stupidity depend on your point of view. They're hard to define. Most importantly, if we can't hope to raise the general intelligence of humanity, how can we move forward?

But what if he's right? What if a civilised

period in history is only due to the extent to which all the stupid people put up with and take care of our thinkers? How would that apply to the world now? Although the world's most powerful leader, George Bush, is clearly a dribbling idiot, are we, the masses, equally stupid? It's easy to say no. After all, we have the internet as a tool to communicate. But notice how thinkers are being gradually silenced, despite this outstanding tool.

People who think differently from the masses are being gagged in America. They're being gagged by a right-wing Christian power. We haven't seen this for years. Since Salman Rushdie's terrible ordeal in the 1980s, no one, however bold, dares to mock Islam for fear of being hounded and killed by thugs. And in the rest of the world religious fundamentalism isn't dying, it's growing in strength like some vile bacteria in a Petrie dish.

None of this points to a golden age. A golden age where the masses think highly of the great thinkers. The photographs of tortured Iraqi prisoners we see now would be familiar to soldiers in 1066. We are bound across the centuries not just by violence and brutality, but by stupidity, which never comes to an end or changes. We are all to blame for letting it happen.

23rd May, 2004

MISSING WOMEN, MISSING RIGHTS

I'm a British woman. There are some rights I don't have yet. Being a submariner in the Royal Navy, or joining the Royal and Ancient Golf Club, are two. Both of them would be too dreadful even to think about, anyway. I suppose at least the first one has some useful purpose. All my other rights are equal to those of men. But like most free Western women, I take none of this for granted.

In 1913, the suffragette Emily Davison died protesting for women's votes. She threw herself in front of the King's horse at the Derby. Since then, the fight for women to become equal with the other 50% of the population has been hard won. In 1918 property-owning females over age 30 were allowed to vote. However, it took until 1928 before all British women were allowed to vote. As recently as 1948 Cambridge University finally let women take full degrees. Until then, women students had been banned from sitting final exams, despite being allowed to attend courses. Unbelievably, it was not until 1953 that women teachers won the right to equal pay with male teachers. It was in a horribly recent 1970 that the Equal Pay Act was passed.

So where are we now? Presumably the fighting for such a basic right, that of being equal, is over and done with. But let's consider this for a moment. The BBC news website has a section called Have Your Say. Last week's question was on 'honour' killings. It asked whether police are doing enough. Scotland Yard has decided to examine files going back 10 years. They contain more than 100 cases in England and Wales that they believe have the sniff of the honour killing about them. They say they just want to 'learn more about the scale and nature of honour killings', but not to re-open the cases. So it seems the answer is a resounding 'no'. The police are not doing enough.

These women are from other cultures. So perhaps the police have decided that it would be insensitive to go poking around in the past. It would be insensitive, in some cases, to find out if these missing women were in fact murdered. But some of these women are from families who gave very weak reasons why they had disappeared off the face of the earth. Those families were keen to tell the police that it had nothing to do with the fact that the missing women were acting outside their culture or religion.

Answers like that would send Inspector Morse into a flat spin for months. But it seems that our real boys in blue were in no hurry to get involved in one cultural belief: women who do not do as they are told deserve to die.

This is a BBC website. The public can use it free, but it is regularly checked. So it is largely free of internet nutters. But on this issue, one comment posted by a member of the public was chilling. Ibrahim from London has this to say about 'honour killings':

'This is part of our culture! Westerners don't understand the concept of honour, and don't respect our ways. How can you say you're tolerant?'

Ibrahim doesn't say who 'we' might be. From

his location it seems he is a British citizen. Is this why our police are reluctant to re-open suspicious cases? Are they in agreement with Ibrahim? Do they not understand the concept of non-Western honour? Perhaps they are frightened it will look as if they do not respect Ibrahim's 'ways' until they 'learn more about the scale and nature of honour killings'?

This is an example of how muddled thinking about different cultures in this country has led to a terrible abuse of women's rights in modern times. There are very few ethnic groups who think honour killings are acceptable. But this means that British women who happen to be born into these groups don't have the same rights as other British women.

The police are clearly unwilling to re-open these 10-year-old cases. But compare this to another case. Look at the way the force investigated the murder of Arlene Fraser in Aberdeen, not once letting go. This was another 'honour' killing. A violent and amoral man hired a hit-man to kill a woman for not obeying and respecting him. He killed her, in effect, for bringing him dishonour. He wished to avoid the cost of a divorce settlement. More importantly, he wanted to make sure she would never be able to have a new life with another man. No body was found. And there are no bodies in many of the cases discussed at a recent Europol conference in The Hague. At this conference, European police discussed how to deal with the growing number of 'honour' killings.

In Fraser's case, the police kept going until they got their man. So why was Arlene Fraser different from those 65 or more other British women? For her, the police worked hard to bring her killer to justice. Was it because she was white?

I have known many Muslims - friends and people I have worked with. In my entire life, from primary school onwards, I have never met one single person who thought honour killing was in any way acceptable. It is not part of Muslim culture. It is the warped fantasy of barbarians. If the police are afraid they will be accused of being racist if they re-open cases, then they should think again. It is not just racism itself, but appalling sexism, to treat these suspicious cases differently. And as for Ibrahim from London, he should be grateful for our tolerance. Or we might think of coming round with the girls and punching his lights out.

27th June, 2004

WHY MATERNITY PAY SHOULD HAVE A CORD ATTACHED

Anyone who says they haven't lied is a liar. I lied in the summer between leaving school and starting art college. I'm still ashamed. Student jobs at the time were scarce, but there were plenty of full-time jobs for school leavers. Of course this was a very long time ago. Dinosaurs were just dying out and Americans were popular.

So I got a job as a trainee assistant in a jewellery store in Glasgow's East End. As holiday jobs go it was ok. Over four months I was trained to sell worthless junk to working-class women, who really believed that spending their precious wages on nine-carat gold gate bracelets was a real investment. They didn't understand that the bracelets were almost worthless the moment the velvet box was snapped shut. At 17, I didn't have to think about that.

I was good at selling this tat. I told my gullible customers that it was a sensible use of their money. I even pretended to admire the ugly golden cuffs. I clipped them onto their chubby wrists like shackles, and they were the wage slaves. I was the one who had to lock the rings in the safe. I even set the alarm and locked up the shop. I worked hard and I was reliable. At one point the beaming owner invited me into his office and told me I could be a manager one day.

Well done everyone.

The only problem was that I was a liar. I knew all along that I was leaving in September to start first year at art college. When I told him I was leaving the manager went into a fit of rage. He would have to begin looking for someone else, and begin training all over again. What did I care? I was off to draw nudes and drink cheap beer. But I do care now. I'm still ashamed of that, and it came back to haunt me with the recent fuss over maternity rights.

One in four British employers doesn't think it's worth training a pregnant woman. No surprises there. But it raises all kinds of ugly ideas, not least the eternal one of sexism. Naturally voices have been raised on all sides.

Working mothers and feminists are angry at the implications for Britain's workplace. Some childless workers are irritated by the rights given to working mothers but not to them. Many employers are staying quiet. They know they will continue to discriminate, as and when they choose, with little chance of being caught. Older women, who had to balance work and motherhood without any kind of state help, are angry about the hardship they had to face. But they hide it by tut-tutting over modern women and their dilemma.

All this conflict starts up again every time an issue to do with working and parenting raises its head and the debate grinds on once again.

So what has my stint in a jewellery store, when I was young and childless, got to do with all this? It seems to me that there is one fundamental point missing from the whole maternity debate. Honesty. Of course some employers are dishonest when they say they have chosen a male employee over a female one because the man performs better. It's not just about being afraid of paying someone who goes off to have children, they say. However, there are just as many dishonest women who take maternity benefits knowing full well, as I did in my jewellery shop job, that they are never coming back.

What seems astonishing is that this entire conflict could be solved with one simple change in the law. It would put a stop to the system being abused. It would ensure that women and employers are equally protected. Then the opportunity for mothers to be regarded as good employment bets would be restored.

What is this simple change in the law? Just this. If you take maternity pay and don't return to work, then you pay the money back. How could that be simpler? Maternity pay is not a benefit for having children and contributing to society. That's what child benefit is for. Nor is maternity pay available to all mothers. It is available only to working ones. Maternity pay is designed for one thing and one thing only, and that's to allow working women to continue in employment after childbirth. It protects their right to return. It's an absolutely essential law to ensure equality. Without it women would have almost no chance at all of keeping and building a career, never mind even hanging on to the most menial of jobs to pay the bills.

But many women take the pay with no intention of returning to work. They're the ones who make perfectly sensible laws a constant source of resentment.

Ensuring that women who fail to return to work pay the whole amount back could put a stop to this. Of course allowances could be made for women who become ill and are unable to return. A minimum time limit of a year back at work would mean women could resign after 12 months if coping with childcare and work proves too difficult. But it would grant the employer a guarantee that they would return and it would give mothers a clear choice. Accept the pay and accept the responsibility to return to work that goes with it. Women could pay back the money if they change their minds, or simply leave work in an honest manner without accepting maternity pay if they don't intend to work after the birth.

Funding dishonest working women during their pregnancy when non-working ones get nothing has to stop. Repayment is the fairest solution for everyone.

Sexist employers are rightly being monitored and checked. But women deceiving the employer and the taxpayer are equally dishonest. They're also profoundly anti-feminist. I'd apologise to my jewellery shop employer if I could, but the store is long gone. I doubt my deceit was a cause of this, but you can never be sure.

15th August, 2004

Published with this volume

BLOOD RED ROSES
Lin Anderson

A Prequel to *Driftnet*
with Forensic Scientist Dr Rhona MacLeod

A hen night in Glasgow leaves the bride-to-be dead on a toilet floor. Her body is twisted, her face a mask of terror. Who would kill a girl just before her wedding? Dr Rhona MacLeod and her team are called in to find out. As they go through the evidence, they find themselves in a world where sex is bought and sold, and more violent death is lying in wait.

Lin Anderson is a crime novelist and screenwriter. Her first novel, *Driftnet*, became a Scottish bestseller in August 2003 and has since sold to Germany, France and Russia. *Blood Red Roses* is a prequel to *Driftnet*.
Lin lives in Edinburgh, with her husband, John. She has two sons and one daughter.

GATO
Margaret Elphinstone

An unusual love story set in the Middle Ages, Gato is the story of a young child brought up in a mill. The quiet hardworking lives of the people at the mill are disturbed by the arrival of a wandering Spanish Friar. What is going on between the miller and his wife, and the Friar? The child at the centre of the story tries to understand. The only creatures the child is close to are the mill cats. After the Friar's stay, there is always one called Gato, Spanish for 'cat'.

Margaret Elphinstone has written six other novels, four of which are historical. She began writing in Shetland in the 1970s. As well as being a writer she has worked as a gardener, library assistant, home help and lecturer. She now lives in Glasgow and is Professor of Writing at the University of Strathclyde. She has two daughters.

Also available

THE CHERRY SUNDAE COMPANY
Isla Dewar

THE BLUE HEN
Des Dillon

THE WHITE CLIFFS
Suhayl Saadi

Moira Forsyth, *Series Editor for the Sandstone Vistas, writes:*

The Sandstone Vista Series of books has been developed for readers who are not used to reading full length novels, or for those who simply want to enjoy a 'quick read' which is satisfying and well written.